SOAK YOUR NUTS

KARYN'S CONSCIOUS COMFORT FOODS

RAW RECIPES

Karyn Calabrese

BOOK PUBLISHING COMPANY
Summertown, Tennessee

dedication

This book is dedicated to my son, Dino,
my mother, Marilyn, my grandmother, Hazel,
and my great-grandmother, Claudia.
Without their guidance and life lessons,
I would not have learned so quickly.

to Dino, Marilyn, Hazel & Claudia

contents

acknowledgments

None of us would be enjoying this full, natural, fearless life
without the work and dedication of two tireless, brilliantly intuitive souls,
Dr. Ann Wigmore and Viktoras Kulvinskas. Their research and
dedication to promoting this life-sustaining message is the reason
I enjoy disease-free, youthful vitality.

enjoy this full, natural, fearless life

introduction

For more than thirty years, I have enjoyed near-perfect health. I thrive on an average of four hours of

sleep a night. I run five businesses, and I'm often mistaken for someone twenty years younger without

having ever used Botox or cosmetic surgery. I've healed myself from allergies, physical injuries, poor

eyesight, chronic fatigue, even major dental surgery without ever having visited a doctor's office or taken

so much as an aspirin.

You may be wondering if I am some super-human, genetically gifted individual, but nothing could be further from the truth. In fact, all the women in my family died young and overweight. I have been lucky enough to have been led down a unique path and to have found teachers who helped me discover the secrets to the true fountain of youth, secrets that are available to all of us no matter our background or genetic makeup.

After years of running restaurants and experimenting in my kitchen at home, I am so excited to share some of the raw recipes that have been the key to my success on this journey. I congratulate you on your own decision to explore raw foods. It's certainly not the path of least resistance, but the rewards are well worth the efforts.

More than thirty years of personal experience, research, and health counseling have proven to me that a raw-food diet truly is the way that God and nature intended us to eat. No matter your experience or what piqued your curiosity, I'm sure you've heard some of the buzz about this "trendy new" diet being touted by celebrities and the occasional enlightened doctor. Let me tell you, there's nothing new about it. This is the oldest diet on the planet and the way that human beings were meant to nourish their bodies. I believe it is only by cooking and overprocessing our food that we begin to suffer from the dramatic degeneration and diseases that seem to plague us.

The human body is an amazing machine. Its tissues regenerate every three months and its cells, every seven years. Our bodies are designed to heal themselves of everything from a minor cut to a major illness. However, our bodies will only be as effective as we make them. Bad food choices, stress, and the chemicals in our environment tax our systems, and our cells no longer regenerate as efficiently. I have just as much stress in my life as anyone else, and, living in a city, I am exposed to my share of toxins and chemicals. Yet, thanks to a raw-food diet and regular detoxification, stress and chemicals don't seem to affect me on a cellular level, and my immune system stays strong, my mind clear, and my body, pain-free.

Have you ever noticed that after a big meal—particularly one consisting of meat, dairy, and heavy cooked foods—you feel tired, less sharp, even moody? That's because a large amount of your body's resources are being devoted to digestion, and there's less oxygen circulating to your brain and your cells. Our digestive system is so busy trying to break down foods it was never meant to process that our other systems have less chance to help us heal, and to fight stress, free radicals, and toxins. Now imagine this happening every day for a year, five years, ten years, thirty years. It's no wonder one in every two people in our lifetime will develop cancer or another degenerative disease.

A raw vegan diet doesn't put the same burden on your body. One of the other main benefits of a raw diet is the alkalizing effect it has on our bodies. Our bodies are constantly working to stay alkalized, because an alkaline body means more oxygen in our blood and higher resistance to diseases that can't survive in an alkaline environment. Meat, animal products, and most cooked foods are acidic and immediately contribute to imbalance in our bodies.

Now that we've eliminated a lot from our diets in order to enjoy the rewards of a raw-food lifestyle, let's talk about all the food that not only fuels our bodies but is pretty darn delicious too!

MAKING IT WORK

Many people fail at eating raw because they try to live on salads and carrot sticks. The human body needs salt, fat, and sugar. The key to my success all these years has been to infuse my diet with flavor and passion as well as a balance of nutrients. With some inspiration from my teachers and a lot of creativity, I have created thousands of recipes for uncooked versions of the foods we all grew up on and love. Some of my original and still most popular dishes include ravioli, lasagne, burritos, chili, and even ice cream. Over the years I've served raw versions of nachos, falafel, cupcakes, pad thai, "egg" salad sandwiches, tiramisu, ceviche, chocolate fondue, tamales, deep-dish pizza. . . the list is endless. By utilizing a few simple tools—a blender, juicer, food processor, and dehydrator—you too can create these delicious raw recipes in your home kitchen.

So if a raw diet is so amazing, why do I even bother to open cooked-food restaurants and write a book half full of cooked recipes? My method has always been to be approachable, to meet people where they are, and to give them a bridge into the raw world. What I've learned from the thousands of people I've taught over the past thirty years is that an all-or-nothing approach rarely works, and that few people are going to be 100 percent raw despite their best intentions.

This book is meant to offer the best of both worlds for whatever fits your life at the moment. You might eat raw for breakfast and lunch and cooked for dinner, or raw during the week and cooked on the weekends, or raw for yourself and cooked for your family. Whatever it is, I want you to have the convenience of raw and cooked vegan recipes all in one place. Just flip the book back and forth, and you will always have flexible options at your fingertips.

TRANSITION TIPS

Like many endeavors in our lives, most of us cannot go from A to Z overnight. "Going raw" is a process, and expecting immediate perfection will almost always lead to failure. I've seen it time and time again—people start a raw diet and experience all the wonderful benefits, then as soon as they can't follow the diet perfectly, they fall off the wagon completely and often go back to meat, dairy, and junk food. Our world is not set up to support a raw diet, and it requires a little bit of extra effort and dedication for those who do it.

I encourage you to not aim for perfection but to just try and elevate your experience with food. If you can't always eat raw, try and stick to a vegan diet. If you eat animal products, choose free-range and organic foods. And if worse comes to worst, and you stop at a fast-food place and eat a big cheeseburger, remember there's no reason to beat yourself up over it. It's all part of your process. There's no reason you can't start the next day with a big green smoothie.

Some of these tips from my thirty years of experience may inspire you on your journey:

- Find a support network. Involve friends and family on your journey. Share recipes and hold potluck dinners. Hosting a raw-food Meetup group and starting my business helped me stick to a raw diet.

- Start your day with a satisfying raw breakfast. For me, the best way to start the day is with a delicious green smoothie. That way, I have a filling breakfast that gives me energy and motivates me to keep eating raw all day long.

- Set a different dietary goal each morning. Even if you don't stick to it 100 percent, chances are you will eat more healthfully than you would have normally. For example, if I decide to go a day without sugar, sometimes I'm completely successful. Other times, stress at work may cause me to break down and reach for something sweet, but most of the time, I'll make a good choice, such as an apple or banana, instead of a whole cake.

- Add variety to your diet. Try not to eat the same foods every day and at every meal. Experiment with new recipes. Variety is the spice of life.

- Eat locally grown foods in season as much as possible. Nature knows what's best for our bodies. That is why vegetables with less water content, such as carrots, beets, and turnips, grow in cooler temperatures—they are more suitable for us during the winter.

The women in my classes often tell me how difficult it is to change their family's eating habits. Plus, they say they don't have time to make separate meals for their non-raw family members. Some tips:

- Start your family's journey to raw foods with dessert. I've met very few people who can resist carob pecan cake, strawberry ice cream, or lemon squares.

- Don't tell them it's healthful food. Let the flavors speak for themselves.

- Introduce them to a variety of recipes.

- Many raw recipes can be adapted from cooked recipes. Soak your nuts and grains and use them in raw recipes for yourself while cooking them for your family. It's usually just one or two extra steps.

- Reward your kids for staying healthy. Find a way to reward them for every day they don't have to take a sick day from school.

One of the most frequent complaints I hear is that a raw food diet is expensive. I think a raw diet can be quite inexpensive—especially if you consider that it's an investment in your health. But a raw diet doesn't have to cost you more. Here are some suggestions to keep the costs down:

- Shop at farmer's markets whenever possible for lower prices than most grocery stores.

- Buy seeds, nuts, and grains in bulk from local health food stores or online retailers and sprout at home.

- Balance more expensive, nut-heavy dishes with less expensive grain and veggie dishes.

Taking care of your body needs to be a budget priority. The money you spend now on food will save money in the long run on medicine and doctors' visits.

equipment for a raw kitchen

There's no need to run out and spend a fortune on new kitchen equipment in order to start preparing raw food at home. However, as you delve further into raw foods, there are several great tools that will allow you to create a wider variety of recipes. Stocking your kitchen with a few of these essentials will help you stick with your raw-foods lifestyle once you see how fun, easy, and flavorful it can be.

HIGH-POWERED BLENDER

This is probably the most essential piece of equipment you can purchase for fast and easy raw food preparation. A great blender isn't cheap, but it is a purchase you will not regret. These blenders are powerful enough to purée soups, smoothies, and sauces without having to do a lot of chopping. They are also great for making such desserts as ice cream, chocolate sauce, sweet cream, and pudding. And they last forever; I've had my blender for more than thirty years. The best part: Cleanup is a cinch. Just be sure to buy a blender with a variable-speed dial so you have control over the power.

DEHYDRATOR

By drying foods at temperatures below 118 degrees F, you can create raw cookies, crackers, breads, pie crusts, and more without losing nutritional value. This is a wonderful tool if you are craving crispy textures and food with a "cooked" consistency. Dehydrators are great for drying fruit, making chips, and preserving food. I believe that there never has to be waste in a raw-food kitchen because just about everything can be dehydrated. I even dehydrate leftover soups and pâtés into crackers or leftover salads into a crispy snack mix.

In order to make crackers and other recipes that start with a lot of liquid, you will also want to purchase nonstick dehydrator sheets. These flexible, reusable sheets fit over your dehydrator trays and make it simple to remove food from the trays. Plus, like blenders, cleanup's a snap.

By the way, do not feel you have to stick with the dehydrating times in the recipes, especially the recipes for snacks. The longer foods are dehydrated, the crispier they become, so dehydrating times really depend on how crispy or crunchy you'd like them to be.

FOOD PROCESSOR

Food processors are great timesavers. I usually use a food processor to chop vegetables to get evenly cut pieces in no time at all. A food processor is also a great tool when making pâtés and desserts.

MANDOLINE

An easy and efficient way to get thin, even slices of vegetables and fruit without using a knife is to rely on this old-fashioned but practical tool. It's great for making chips out of sweet potatoes, apples, and beets and slicing turnips for ravioli or zucchini ribbons for lasagne.

SPIRALIZER

Spiralizers, also called spiral slicers, are great tools for getting long, thin pieces out of vegetables. I use a spiralizer to make zucchini noodles for raw "pasta" dishes. (A serrated peeler also would do the trick.) A spiralizer with variable settings can also be used in place of a mandoline to slice vegetables and make chips.

JUICER

Juicers separate liquids from the fibrous pulp of fruits, vegetables, and nuts. Drinking fresh fruit and vegetable juice is a wonderful way to get lots of nutrients without any stress on your digestive system. However, unless you plan to juice regularly at home or delve more deeply into raw-food preparation, a juicer is not an essential piece of equipment; the home cook can achieve the same results with a blender and food processor.

If you do decide to invest in a juicer, I recommend a double-auger juicer as opposed to a single-auger or suction juicer. A double-auger juicer works more slowly to separate liquid and pulp, and I believe the nutrients in the food stay vital longer as a result.

Most of these items are available for sale on my website: karynraw.com.

AGAVE NECTAR: A sweetener made from the agave plant (the same plant from which tequila is made), agave is frequently used in vegan and raw desserts as a substitute for honey. It has a milder taste than honey or maple syrup that won't influence the flavor of a recipe as much. You will find light, amber, and dark varieties of agave nectar. The darker the variety, the more intense the flavor will be.

BRAGG LIQUID AMINOS: Bragg Liquid Aminos is a protein concentrate derived from soybeans. It adds flavor and essential amino acids to almost any dish, and can be used as a substitute for soy sauce and tamari. Look for it in supermarkets and natural food stores.

CAROB: Carob is the fruit from the carob tree. It has a flavor very similar to chocolate and is often used in vegan baking in place of chocolate by people looking to avoid caffeine. Since carob is naturally sweeter than cacao, you may find that it requires less sugar to sweeten recipes made with carob. I make several carob desserts in my restaurants. I think it has a great flavor, but diehard chocolate lovers may not think it quite does the trick. Carob powder and carob chips are available in most natural food stores and in some larger grocery stores.

CHOCOLATE (CACAO): The raw ingredient in all chocolate products is cacao, which is by nature vegan. Chocolate only becomes nonvegan when dairy products are added. When using chocolate to bake or add to recipes, check the ingredients to make sure there is no dairy, or buy chocolate that is labeled vegan.

FLAXSEEDS: Rich in fiber, protein, and omega-3 fatty acids, flaxseeds have been shown to help lower cholesterol and may prevent certain types of cancer. Grinding flaxseeds before use improves digestion and increases nutrient absorption. However, some people prefer the crunch and texture from whole flaxseeds. If you are eliminating eggs from a recipe, you can use 1 tablespoon of ground flaxseeds with 3 tablespoons of warm water to replace each egg.

MACA ROOT POWDER: High in phytochemicals and minerals, this powder is derived from the maca root. When mixed with water, it is used as an herbal coffee substitute.

NAMA SHOYU: Nama shoyu is a type of soy sauce that is raw and unpasteurized. It has a more delicate and complex flavor than cooked and processed soy sauce. Nama shoyu can be purchased at natural food stores.

HONEY: Honey is one of the more controversial ingredients I use in my recipes. Many vegans don't eat honey because they consider it an animal product, so if you prefer, substitute another sweetener, such as agave nectar.

MILK SUBSTITUTES: Most people these days are familiar with soy milk. However, there are many great milk substitutes on the market, including rice milk, hempseed milk, almond milk, and coconut milk. In general, these are interchangeable in any recipe that calls for nondairy milk. Milk substitutes are easy to make at home.

NORI: Nori is thin sheets of pressed seaweed ranging in color from dark green to black and used to wrap sushi, or, when cut into very thin strips, used as a garnish or flavoring.

NUTRITIONAL YEAST FLAKES: An inactive yeast that has a nutty, cheesy flavor, nutritional yeast is often used in vegan cooking to produce a cheese-like flavor. Some brands are nutritionally fortified, making them a good dietary source of vitamin B_{12} for vegans.

SALT: I believe in using the highest quality ingredients whenever possible, and this is especially important when it comes to salt. I primarily use Himalayan salt, which is a mineral-rich pink salt mined primarily in Pakistan. There are also many great sea salt options out there (my favorite is Celtic) so use whichever you prefer or have access to. I carry a small bottle of Himalayan salt with me when I travel and eat out at restaurants.

SWEETENERS: Most commercial white sugar is made from cane sugar and believe it or not is often processed with animal bone char to remove color and impurities, including any nutrients and minerals. This will never be labeled on a package so it's best to look for sugars that are labeled vegan or to use alternatives such as agave nectar, beet sugar, date sugar, dehydrated cane juice, honey, maple syrup, and turbinado. The less processed the sugar, the better.

TAMARI: Tamari is a dark sauce made from soybeans. It is similar to soy sauce, but it is thicker and doesn't have the sharp flavor of regular soy sauce. Tamari is used as a condiment or a dipping sauce.

WATER: I recommend using only filtered, purified water in all of your cooking.

breakfast treats

Nut Milk

Milks can be made from almost any seed or nut, so use your favorite or any that you have on hand. Some options are almonds, Brazil nuts, pumpkin seeds, sesame seeds, and sunflower seeds. You'll need cheesecloth or a nut-milk bag, which is a cloth bag made specifically to strain homemade nut milks.

5 cups nuts, seeds, or a combination

10 cups water

1 cup honey or agave nectar (optional)

1 tablespoon vanilla extract

Soak the nuts or seeds in enough water to cover for 2 hours. Drain and rinse.

Put about 1½ cups of the nuts and about 3 cups of fresh water in a blender. Process until the mixture becomes a smooth liquid, stopping occasionally to scrape down the blender jar. Strain the nut mixture through a nut milk bag or several layers of cheesecloth stretched over a large bowl. Repeat until all of the nuts are blended and strained.

Fill half of the blender jar with the nut milk. Add the optional honey and the vanilla extract. Process until well blended. Pour the sweetened nut milk into the bowl with the remaining nut milk and mix well. Stored in a covered container in the refrigerator, Nut Milk will keep for 1 week.

NOTE: The pulp is what is left after making nut milk. If you are using almonds in this recipe to make almond milk, reserve 2½ cups of the pulp to make Almond-Berry Muffins (page 16).

Chocolate Milkshakes

YIELD: 4 SERVINGS

This chocolate shake will satisfy any sweet tooth.

1 cup coconut butter or chopped avocado

2 avocados, chopped

½ cup honey or agave nectar

2 teaspoons bee pollen (optional)

1 teaspoon vanilla extract

2 cups Nut Milk (page 10) **or prepared vegan milk of your choice**

1 cup raw cacao powder

1 cup ice cubes

Put the coconut butter, avocados, honey, the optional bee pollen, and vanilla extract in a blender. Process until smooth, stopping occasionally to scrape down the blender jar. Add the Nut Milk, cacao, and ice. Process again until smooth. Serve immediately. Stored in a covered container in the refrigerator, Chocolate Milkshakes will keep for 1 week.

Soak Your Nuts

Nuts contain natural compounds that prevent them from sprouting prematurely. Soaking breaks down these compounds and begins the sprouting process, which I believe makes nuts easier to digest. An added bonus is that it may increase the absorption of their nutrients. I feel satisfied more quickly and am likely to eat fewer nuts if I've soaked them first. This applies to seeds, grains, and legumes as well.

I always have several jars of soaked nuts in my refrigerator ready for a quick snack or to use in a recipe. Nuts can be dried at room temperature or in a dehydrator to return them to their presoaked crunchiness.

Soak nuts in a bowl in enough water to cover and follow recipe instructions. If you have time, soak them overnight, or use this general guide.

NUT OR SEED	SOAK TIME
Almonds	8 hours or overnight
Brazil nuts	1 to 2 hours
Cashews	1 to 2 hours
Pecans	2 to 4 hours
Sesame seeds	30 minutes
Sunflower seeds	30 minutes
Walnuts	2 to 4 hours

Some recipes also will call for some soaked grains, such as quinoa, rice, and wheat. This requires a little more prep work, but it's an easy process and the rewards are well worth it. (Just follow recipe instructions.) I actually find it pretty amazing that a little water and a few days' time can bring these grains to life.

The Buddha

YIELD: 2 SERVINGS

This smoothie is great after a workout. The minerals and electrolytes in coconut water will replenish and hydrate your body, and the natural sugar in the honey and apple juice will give you energy.

¾ cup apple juice

¾ cup coconut water

½ cup ice cubes

1 to 2 tablespoons tahini

1 teaspoon honey

1 teaspoon lemon juice

1 teaspoon spirulina or kamut (optional)

Put all of the ingredients in a blender. Process until smooth.

How to Sprout

You can significantly increase beans' digestibility by sprouting them before they're cooked, because the sprouting process breaks down many of the heavy starches that cause digestive discomfort.

Sprouting is easy. Just soak dried beans in enough water to cover for 8 hours. Drain and rinse. Repeat the soaking, draining, and rinsing every 12 hours, just until the beans begin to sprout. In most cases, this will take 2 or 3 days. The beans are sprouted when they crack and begin to grow a "tail." They also will be soft enough to bite into. (This method also works for sprouting the wheat berries for the Rejuvelac recipe on page 13.)

Sprouted beans take less time to cook than dried beans. Plan on cooking sprouted beans about 35 minutes.

Rejuvelac

Rejuvelac is instant energy—the "Gatorade" of the health-conscious—taken for its full complex of B vitamins and its ability to develop friendly bacteria in the digestive tract. I drink it plain, but it also makes a great base for other beverages.

¾ cup sprouted wheat berries (see How to Sprout, page 12)

8 cups water, plus more to blend wheat berries

DAY 1: Put the wheat berries in a blender. Add enough water to cover the berries by 2 inches. Process for 20 seconds, or until the wheat berries are ground but still have some texture. (They should be grainy but not a fine powder.) Transfer the mixture to a large bowl. Add the remaining 8 cups of water. Cover the bowl with a piece of cheesecloth or paper towel. Let stand overnight at room temperature.

DAY 2: Stir the mixture with a spoon for 5 to 10 seconds. Cover. Let stand overnight at room temperature.

DAY 3: Repeat Day 2.

DAY 4: Strain the mixture through a fine-mesh strainer into glass jars. Stored in covered containers, Rejuvelac will keep for 2 weeks.

NOTE: Reserve the strained wheat berries for Wheat Berry Crackers (page 69).

Rejuvenating Juleps

YIELD: 2 CUPS

A new, high-energy twist on a Southern classic.

2 cups mint leaves

1½ cups Rejuvelac (page 13)

¼ cup honey

½ lime, unpeeled

Put all of the ingredients in a blender. Process for about 10 seconds, stopping occasionally to scrape down the blender jar. Serve in a cocktail glass.

Karyn's Granola

YIELD: 5 CUPS

This granola is great for breakfast or as a snack. Crumble it over oatmeal or a parfait. Add nut milk or simply eat it as is. Make a big batch. Stored in a tightly covered container, it will keep for six months to one year.

3 cups rolled oats

½ cup almonds

½ cup pecans

½ cup raisins

½ cup walnuts

2 tablespoons ground cinnamon

¾ cup agave nectar or honey

2 tablespoons vanilla extract

Combine the oats, almonds, pecans, raisins, walnuts, and cinnamon in a large bowl. Add the agave nectar and vanilla extract. Stir until all the ingredients are well coated. Pour the mixture evenly into the dehydrator trays. Dehydrate at 118 degrees F for about 5 hours. Stir the mixture to prevent it from sticking to the trays. Dehydrate for another 4 to 6 hours, or until the mixture reaches the desired texture and crunchiness.

Almond-Berry Muffins

See photo facing page 68.

YIELD: 12 MUFFINS

Keep these muffins around for breakfast or as a snack. This recipe calls for almond pulp, which is what is left over after making Nut Milk (page 10) with almonds. (Nothing is wasted in a raw-food kitchen.)

2½ cups almond pulp or ground almonds

1¼ cups pecans

1¼ cups walnuts

2½ cups rolled oats

1 cup agave nectar

2 cups dried cranberries or blueberries

½ cup coconut butter

¼ cup plus 1 tablespoon ground cinnamon

1 tablespoon vanilla extract

Line a muffin pan with paper cupcake cups. Set aside.

Put the almond pulp, pecans, and walnuts in a blender. Process into small pieces. Transfer mixture to a large bowl.

Put the oats in the blender. Process into a fine meal. Transfer the oats and all the remaining ingredients to the bowl with the nut mixture. Stir until well combined.

Form the dough into 12 balls and place them in the prepared pan. Dehydrate at 118 degrees F for 12 hours for soft moist muffins or longer for crunchier muffins.

ALMOND-CARROT MUFFINS: Substitute 1 cup peeled, shredded carrots and 1 cup raisins for the dried cranberries or blueberries.

Sprouted Wheat Toast

YIELD: 16 SERVINGS

Serve this tasty toast with Creamy Strawberry Jelly (page 18).

2 cups sesame seeds

4 cups spring wheat berries, sprouted (see How to Sprout, page 12)

1 cup water

¼ cup raisins

¼ cup sunflower oil

1 teaspoon ground cinnamon

1 teaspoon sea salt

3 dates, pitted and chopped

1 cup flaxseeds

Soak the sesame seeds in enough water to cover for 8 hours. Drain and rinse in a fine-mesh strainer. Put them in a food processor with the wheat berries, water, raisins, oil, cinnamon, salt, and dates. Process until smooth, stopping occasionally to scrape down the work bowl. Transfer to a medium bowl. Fold in the flaxseeds.

Line the dehydrator trays with nonstick dehydrator sheets. Transfer the mixture to the sheets and spread to the desired thickness. Dehydrate at 115 degrees F for 4 hours. Flip the mixture onto the trays. Dehydrate for another 6 hours. Cut the bread into 16 pieces. Wrapped and refrigerated, Sprouted Wheat Toast will keep for 3 months. Bring to room temperature before serving.

Creamy Strawberry Jelly

YIELD: 3 CUPS

This tasty concoction turns into a jelly when it's refrigerated. Keep it around for breakfast or a snack. You can make a great sandwich with this jelly, almond butter, and the White Bread on page 70.

3 cups frozen strawberries, thawed

½ cup agave nectar

1½ teaspoons psyllium seeds

Put the strawberries plus any juice they have released, the agave nectar, and the psyllium seeds in a blender. Process until smooth and creamy, stopping occasionally to scrape down the blender jar. Stored in a covered container in the refrigerator, Creamy Strawberry Jelly will keep for 2 weeks.

NOTE: Whenever you have fresh strawberries that are a bit too ripe, don't throw them away. Put them in a plastic bag in the freezer until you have enough for this delicious jelly.

Apple-Raisin Oatmeal

YIELD: 4 SERVINGS

This is a sweet, healthful way to start your day. You can prepare it in advance, and store it in the refrigerator, and you'll only have to make it once a week.

- 3 cups rolled oats
- 2 cups apple juice
- 2 cups water
- ¾ cup raisins
- 3 tablespoons agave nectar
- ¼ red apple, diced
- ¼ green apple, diced

Combine the oats, juice, water, raisins, and agave nectar in a medium bowl. Mix well. Divide evenly among four serving bowls and sprinkle each with some red and green apple.

salads, dressings, and condiments

CHAPTER 2

Curried Cauliflower Salad

YIELD: 4 SERVINGS

This salad will satisfy your curry craving.

¾ cup cashews

½ cup water

3 tablespoons olive oil

2 tablespoons curry powder

1 head cauliflower, broken into bite-sized florets

1 cup combination of diced green, red, yellow, and orange bell peppers

½ cup chopped red onion

Sea salt

Soak the cashews in enough water to cover for 6 hours. Drain. Transfer the cashews to a blender with ½ cup of fresh water, the oil, and curry powder. Process until smooth and creamy.

Put the cauliflower, bell peppers, and onion in a medium bowl. Add the curry dressing and toss well. Season with salt to taste.

Italian Sprouted-Bean Salad

YIELD: 7 CUPS; 14 SERVINGS

This salad is great for parties and picnics. For instructions on sprouting beans, see How to Sprout on page 12.

1 cup sun-dried tomatoes (not oil-packed)
1 cup dried adzuki beans, sprouted
1 cup dried black beans, sprouted
1 cup dried garbanzo beans, sprouted
1 cup dried lentils, sprouted
1 cup chopped baby spinach
½ cup extra-virgin olive oil
Pinch sea salt, plus more to taste
1 cup chopped kalamata olives
¼ cup chopped garlic
¼ cup honey or sweetener of your choice

Soak the tomatoes in enough water to cover for 1 hour. Drain. Set aside.

Combine the beans, lentils, spinach, ¼ cup of the oil, and a pinch of salt in a large bowl. Mix well. With your hands or a large spoon, mix in the tomatoes, olives, and garlic. Add the honey and mix again. Stir in the remaining ¼ cup of oil. Season with salt to taste.

Asian Paradise Salad

YIELD: 4 SERVINGS

Make sure you use sunflower sprouts, not sprouted sunflower seeds. You can have fun with this salad and serve it on a leaf of red cabbage.

- **2 cups alfalfa sprouts**
- **2 cups shredded beets**
- **2 cups shredded carrots**
- **⅓ cup sunflower sprouts**
- **Asian Paradise Dressing** (page 24)

Combine the alfalfa sprouts, beets, carrots, and sunflower sprouts in a large bowl. Mix well. Serve with Asian Paradise Dressing.

Asian Paradise Dressing

YIELD: 2 CUPS

This is the perfect dressing for a sensational summer salad.

1 ½ cups lemon juice

½ cup honey

¼ cup tamari or nama shoyu

2 tablespoons sesame oil

2 ½ teaspoons ground ginger

Put all the ingredients in a blender. Process until well blended. Stored in a covered container in the refrigerator, Asian Paradise Dressing will keep for 1 month. Shake well before serving.

Papaya-Avocado Fruit Salad

YIELD: 3 SERVINGS

This salad is perfect for breakfast, lunch, or dinner. Garnish with shredded dried coconut for an added tropical touch.

> **2 bananas, sliced**
>
> **1 papaya, diced**
>
> **1 avocado, diced**
>
> **Juice of 1 lime**
>
> **3 tablespoons chopped macadamia nuts or other nuts**

Gently combine the bananas, papaya, and avocado in a medium bowl; avoid mashing the fruit. Pour the lime juice over the fruit, and sprinkle with the nuts. Toss gently.

Sweet Spinach Salad

YIELD: 3 SERVINGS

Spinach is highly nutritious and is extremely rich in antioxidants. This is a delicious way to eat a nutrient-packed meal.

4 cups baby spinach

1 red apple, diced

1 red onion, sliced

¼ cup chopped walnuts

¼ cup diced red bell pepper

Sweet Salad Dressing (page 27)

Combine the spinach, apple, onion, walnuts, and bell pepper in a large bowl. Add Sweet Spinach Dressing and toss well.

NOTE: To keep the spinach from wilting, add the dressing just before serving. Or, pass the dressing at the table so each person can dress his salad just before eating it.

Sweet Salad Dressing

YIELD: 3 CUPS

This dressing has the right balance of sweet and sour to spice up any salad.

2 cups olive oil

1 cup pitted dates

¼ cup plus 1 tablespoon cider vinegar

1 tablespoon mustard seeds

3 cloves garlic

1 teaspoon sea salt

Put all the ingredients in a blender. Process until smooth, stopping occasionally to scrape down the blender jar. (The mustard seeds will remain intact.) Stored in a covered container in the refrigerator, Sweet Spinach Dressing will keep for 1 month. Shake well before serving.

Exotic Hempseed Salad

YIELD: 3 SERVINGS

This simple meal packs a lot of protein.

4 cups mixed salad greens

1 avocado, diced

½ cup cherry tomato halves

¼ cup chopped macadamia nuts

3 teaspoons to ¼ cup hempseeds

Hempseed Salad Dressing (page 29)

Combine all the ingredients in a large bowl. Toss gently. Serve with Hempseed Salad Dressing.

Hempseed Salad Dressing

YIELD: 4 CUPS

This dressing goes well with most salads and is heart- and brain-friendly, so don't worry about portion size.

1½ cups olive oil

½ cup chopped beets

½ cup hempseed oil

¼ cup cider vinegar

6 cloves garlic

1 pitted date

1 teaspoon ground ginger

½ teaspoon sea salt

½ teaspoon fennel seeds

Pinch cayenne

Put all the ingredients in a blender. Process until smooth, stopping occasionally to scrape down the blender jar. Stored in a covered container in the refrigerator, Hempseed Salad Dressing will keep for 1 month. Shake well before serving.

Cabbage Salad with Ginger-Miso Dressing

YIELD: 4 SERVINGS

Make this salad a little more colorful by using both green and red cabbage.

¼ cup sea vegetables of your choice

½ green or red cabbage or a combination, shredded or finely chopped

2 carrots, grated

½ cup grated broccoli stems

¼ cup chopped red bell pepper

Ginger-Miso Dressing (page 31)

Soak the sea vegetables in enough water to cover for 15 to 20 minutes. Drain. Chop and transfer them to a large bowl.

Add the cabbage, carrots, broccoli, and bell pepper. Mix well. Serve with Ginger-Miso Dressing.

Ginger-Miso Dressing

This dressing is especially good in the wintertime since ginger helps to make your body feel warm.

1 cup sesame oil

1 cup water

1/2 cup miso

1/3 cup chopped dates

1/4 cup olive oil

1/4 cup sesame seeds

2 tablespoons finely chopped fresh ginger

2 cloves garlic

1 teaspoon sea salt

1/2 teaspoon red pepper flakes

Put all the ingredients in a blender. Process until smooth, stopping occasionally to scrape down the blender jar. Stored in a covered container in the refrigerator, Ginger-Miso Dressing will keep for 1 month. Shake well before serving.

Lemon-Tahini Asparagus Salad

YIELD: 4 SERVINGS

This refreshing salad is lovely on its own or as a side dish to any main course.

DRESSING

2 tablespoons olive oil

1 tablespoon cider vinegar

1 tablespoon lemon juice

1 tablespoon nama shoyu

1 tablespoon tahini

1 teaspoon chopped fresh ginger

1 clove garlic

Pinch cayenne

SALAD

1 pound asparagus, cut into ¼-inch pieces

1 red bell pepper, diced

1 carrot, julienned

1 green onion, chopped

To make the dressing, put all the ingredients in a blender. Process until smooth.

To make the salad, combine all the ingredients in a large bowl. Add the salad dressing and toss well.

Moroccan Carrot Salad

YIELD: 6 SERVINGS

This salad is kid-friendly, and the beautiful orange color will draw attention on any picnic or potluck table.

1 pound carrots, shredded

¼ cup olive oil

5 pitted dates, chopped

Juice of 1 lemon

2 tablespoons chopped fresh mint leaves

1 teaspoon minced fresh ginger

¼ teaspoon ground cloves

Put the shredded carrots in a large bowl and set aside.

Put all the remaining ingredients in a blender. Process until smooth. Add it to the carrots and toss well.

Spicy Cucumber Salad

YIELD: 2 TO 4 SERVINGS

This salad will complement a cooked or raw dish well and send your taste buds into overdrive with its combination of spicy and fresh.

1 pound cucumbers, peeled and sliced

1 red bell pepper, chopped

1 green onion, cut into ¼-inch pieces

2 tablespoons olive oil

2 tablespoons lemon juice

1 tablespoon minced fresh parsley

1 teaspoon chopped jalapeño chile

1 clove garlic, minced

Sea salt

Combine the cucumbers, bell pepper, and green onion in a large bowl and set aside.

Put the oil, lemon juice, parsley, jalapeño, and garlic in a blender. Process until well combined. Add to the salad and toss well. Season with salt to taste.

Crave-Buster Salad

YIELD: 2 SERVINGS

This salad will satisfy and curb any craving. Add Onion Crisps (page 68) as a savory and crunchy topping.

1¼ heads romaine lettuce, chopped

½ cup chopped spinach

¼ cup sunflower sprouts

¼ cup hempseeds

½ avocado, sliced

2 tablespoons grapeseed oil

2 tablespoons olive oil

1 teaspoon lime juice

½ teaspoon sea salt

¼ cup dulse

Combine the romaine, spinach, sprouts, hempseeds, and avocado in a large bowl and set aside.

Mix the grapeseed oil, olive oil, lime juice, and salt in a small bowl. Add it to the salad and toss well. Sprinkle with dulse.

Raw Caesar Dressing

YIELD: 4 CUPS

You will want the dulse to get mixed in with the dressing, but not blended, or the dressing will be dark and not the light-colored dressing with the black specs that we are all used to in traditional Caesar Dressing.

2 cups olive oil

1 cup lemon juice

½ cup Bragg Liquid Aminos

½ cup garlic cloves

½ cup cold water

1½ tablespoons dulse

Put the oil, lemon juice, Bragg Liquid Aminos, garlic, and water in a blender. Process on high speed for 2 minutes, or until smooth. Pour the dressing into a large bowl. Whisk in the dulse until it is evenly distributed. Stored in a covered container in the refrigerator, Raw Caesar Dressing will keep for 1 month. Shake well before serving.

Mustard Vinaigrette

YIELD: ABOUT ⅔ CUP

This dressing brings brussels sprouts to life in the recipe for Carmelized Brussels Sprouts with Mustard Vinaigrette (see Vegan Fare, page 59). In the raw kitchen, it adds spice to just about any salad or side dish.

¼ cup Dijon mustard or brown mustard

¼ cup olive oil

2 tablespoons champagne vinegar

1 teaspoon honey or agave nectar

Sea salt

Freshly ground pepper

Whisk the mustard, oil, vinegar, and honey in a small bowl until combined. Season with salt and pepper to taste. Stored in a covered container in the refrigerator, Mustard Vinaigrette will keep for 1 month. Shake well before serving.

Lemon Dressing

YIELD: 3 1/2 CUPS

Zippy and refreshing, this dressing will quickly become part of your repertoire. It's especially good with fresh mixed greens.

1 cup olive oil

1 cup water

1/2 cup Bragg Liquid Aminos

1/2 cup cider vinegar

1/2 cup lemon juice

1/4 cup garlic cloves

1/4 cup honey

2 1/4 teaspoons dried basil

2 1/4 teaspoons dried dill weed

2 1/4 teaspoons dulse

2 1/4 teaspoons dried oregano

2 1/4 teaspoons dried rosemary

2 1/4 teaspoons sea salt

2 1/4 teaspoons dried thyme

1/2 small bay leaf

Put all the ingredients in a blender. Process for 2 minutes, or until well mixed, stopping occasionally to scrape down the blender jar. Stored in a covered container in the refrigerator, Lemon Dressing will keep for 1 month. Shake well before serving.

Raw Mustard

YIELD: 1¼ CUPS

Don't be put off by the soaking time. This delicious mustard is simple to make, and, once you taste it, it could very well be the last time you buy the bottled stuff.

1 cup brown mustard seeds

1½ cups cider vinegar

1 cup sun-dried tomatoes (not oil-packed)

¼ cup fresh basil leaves

2 tablespoons nama shoyu

Soak the mustard seeds in the cider vinegar for 3 days. Soak the tomatoes in a separate bowl in enough water to cover for 1 day.

Drain the mustard seeds and tomatoes and put them in a food processor with the basil and nama shoyu. Process for 10 minutes, or until smooth. (The mustard seeds will remain intact.) Stored in a covered container in the refrigerator, Raw Mustard will keep for 2 months.

Raw Mayonnaise

YIELD: 2 CUPS

This easy and delicious dressing will keep any sandwich from feeling naked.

1 ¼ cups cashews

¼ cup water

2 tablespoons olive oil

1 stalk celery, chopped

½ teaspoon sea salt

1 clove garlic

Put the cashews, water, and oil in a blender. Process until smooth, stopping occasionally to scrape down the blender jar. Add the remaining ingredients. Process again, on high speed, until smooth and creamy. Stored in a covered container in the refrigerator, Raw Mayonnaise will keep for 2 months.

Raw No-Nut Mayonnaise

YIELD: 2 CUPS

Raw vegan mayonnaise often is a nut-based condiment. This one is for those who can't eat or don't like nuts.

1 cup olive oil

½ cup lime juice

½ cup light miso

4 cloves garlic

½ teaspoon sea salt

Put all the ingredients in a blender. Process on high speed until smooth and creamy. Pour into a glass container, cover, and refrigerate for 2 hours, or until it becomes thick and spreadable. Stored in a covered container in the refrigerator, Raw No-Nut Mayonnaise will keep for 2 months.

Raw Ketchup

YIELD: 3 CUPS

A popular condiment in any kitchen, even a raw one.

1 cup sun-dried tomatoes (not oil-packed)

1 cup chopped fresh tomatoes

¼ cup maple syrup

¼ cup olive oil

¼ cup chopped onion

2 tablespoons minced fresh ginger

8 basil leaves

6 pitted dates

1 tablespoon minced garlic

1 teaspoon salt

Soak the sun-dried tomatoes in enough water to cover for 2 hours. Drain. Transfer them to a food processor with all the remaining ingredients. Process until smooth. Stored in a covered container in the refrigerator, Raw Ketchup will keep for 2 months.

entrées

CHAPTER 3

Fresh Corner Gazpacho

See photo on facing page.

YIELD: 6 SERVINGS

This is one of the most refreshing meals you can eat in the summertime.

5 tomatoes, diced

1 red bell pepper, diced

1 yellow bell pepper, diced

½ cucumber, cubed

½ zucchini, diced

¼ onion, diced

½ cup olive oil

¼ cup chopped fresh parsley

3 tablespoons balsamic vinegar

1 to 2 tablespoons vegetable-salt seasoning

1 tablespoon chopped garlic

Pinch cayenne, plus more to taste

Pinch sea salt, plus more to taste

Put the tomatoes, bell peppers, cucumber, zucchini, and onion in a large bowl. Mix well.

In a medium bowl, combine all the remaining ingredients. Stir until well combined. Pour the parsley mixture into the tomato mixture. Mix well.

Pour 1 cup of the mixture into a blender. Process until smooth, stopping occasionally to scrape down the blender jar. Add back to the bowl with the soup and mix well.

Refrigerate until well chilled. Serve cold. Season with more cayenne and salt to taste.

Fresh Corner Gazpacho, *on facing page*

Stuffed Peppers with Wild Rice and Barley Pilaf, *page 52*

Chillin' Chili

Cold weather can make us crave comfort foods, and there's no food that satisfies that craving like a nice bowl of chili.

2 cups chopped white mushrooms

½ cup olive oil

½ teaspoon salt

3 large tomatoes, chopped

2 green bell peppers, chopped

1 yellow onion, chopped

¼ cup sun-dried tomatoes (not oil-packed)

6 cloves garlic

1 teaspoon cayenne

½ cup black olives

¼ cup Bragg Liquid Aminos

3 tablespoons chili powder

2 teaspoons chopped fresh thyme

3 cups dried adzuki beans, sprouted (see How to Sprout, page 12)

2 avocados, cut into in large chunks

Put the mushrooms, oil, and salt in a medium bowl. Mix well. Let marinate for 30 minutes.

Put the fresh tomatoes, bell peppers, onion, sun-dried tomatoes, garlic, and cayenne in a blender. Process until well blended, stopping occasionally to scrape down the blender jar. Transfer to a large bowl.

Put the olives, Bragg Liquid Aminos, chili powder, and thyme in a food processor. Process until well combined, stopping occasionally to scrape down the work bowl. Transfer to the tomato mixture. Add the beans, mushroom mixture, and avocados and mix well.

Marinate for 2 to 3 hours in the refrigerator before serving.

Spinach-Stuffed Ravioli with Raw Marinara Sauce

YIELD: 4 TO 6 SERVINGS

There's no pasta in this ravioli. No cooking, either. These ravioli are excellent served with the Raw Marinara Sauce (page 55) or with just a drizzle of olive oil.

1 cup cashews

1 cup macadamia nuts

4 cups chopped baby spinach

1 tablespoon olive oil

½ teaspoon sea salt plus more to taste

½ cup lemon juice

2 cloves garlic

2 large turnips, peeled

Raw Marinara Sauce (page 55)

¼ cup olive oil (optional)

Soak the cashews and macadamias in separate bowls in enough water to cover for 2 hours. Put the spinach in a large ziplock bag. Drizzle with 1 tablespoon of the oil and sprinkle with ½ teaspoon of the salt. Gently toss the spinach with your hands. Close the bag and set aside for 10 minutes, or until the spinach is soft.

Drain and rinse the cashews and macadamias. Put them in a food processor with the lemon juice and garlic. Process until smooth, stopping occasionally to scrape down the work bowl. If the mixture seems too thick, add about ½ cup water and process again. Transfer the cashew cheese to a large bowl. Mix in the spinach. Set aside.

To make the ravioli, slice the turnips into very thin rounds on a mandoline or in a food processor. Transfer to a large bowl. Sprinkle a few slices with salt. Gently massage them with your hands to soften them slightly. Repeat until all the turnip slices have been salted and massaged. Cover with plastic wrap and let stand for 5 minutes to soften further.

Put a dollop of the spinach filling in the center of a turnip slice. Fold the slice over to form a ravioli and gently press the edges closed. Repeat with the remaining turnip slices and filling.

Serve the ravioli with the Raw Marinara Sauce or drizzle with the optional olive oil if desired.

Eggless Egg Salad

YIELD: 4 CUPS

Finally, an egg salad that you can take to a picnic and not worry about leaving out in the sun.

2 cups macadamia nuts

½ cup water

1 tablespoon ground turmeric

2½ cups chopped white onions

1 cup chopped coconut meat

¼ cup plus 1 tablespoon chopped celery

Sea salt

Soak the macadamias in enough water to cover for 2 hours. Drain and rinse. Put them in a blender with ¼ cup of the fresh water and the turmeric. Process until smooth, stopping occasionally to scrape down the blender jar. Gradually add the remaining ¼ cup of water as needed until well blended.

Put the onions, coconut, and celery in a large bowl. Pour the macadamia mixture over them. Mix well. Season with salt to taste.

Tuna-free Tuna Salad

YIELD: 4 CUPS

You can make yourself a great tuna sandwich using this salad and the White Bread (page 70).

3 cups Almond Pâté (page 50)
1 cup minced celery
½ cup chopped white onion
2 tablespoons dulse

Combine all the ingredients in a large bowl and mix well.

Almond Pâté

YIELD: 3 CUPS

Pâté is a versatile staple of the raw diet. Change the veggies and seasonings to vary the taste and to create different ethnic recipes.

2 cups almonds

1 tomato (preferably Beefsteak)

¼ cup chopped white onion

3 to 4 tablespoons Bragg Liquid Aminos

2 cloves garlic

¼ teaspoon cayenne

Soak the almonds in enough water to cover for 8 to 12 hours. Drain and rinse. Transfer the almonds to a food processor and pulse several times, until coarsely chopped.

Add the tomato, onion, Bragg Liquid Aminos, garlic, and cayenne. Process into a creamy paste, stopping occasionally to scrape down the work bowl. Stored in a covered glass container in the refrigerator, Almond Pâté will keep for 7 to 10 days. Any leftovers may be spread onto a dehydrator tray and dehydrated at 118 degrees F for 15 hours to make crackers. The crackers will keep indefinitely.

Red Beans and Rice

YIELD: 6 SERVINGS

Not many people would think that you can serve raw rice, but if you use the right kind of rice and soak it, raw rice can be tender and delicious. When soaking rice, use a deep glass container and make sure the rice is completely covered so it doesn't dry out.

2 cups wild rice or brown rice

3 large tomatoes, chopped

2 tablespoons hempseed oil

1 tablespoon olive oil

1 tablespoon sunflower oil

1 small habanero (optional)

2 cups dried aduzki beans, sprouted (see How to Sprout, page 12)

1 cup diced celery

½ avocado, chopped

½ cup diced onion

2 teaspoons ground cumin

½ teaspoon ground coriander

Sea salt

Soak the rice in 3 cups of water in a large bowl overnight. Drain and rinse. Add 3 cups fresh water. Repeat for 4 days.

Put 2 of the tomatoes, oils, and the optional habanero in a food processor. Process until well blended, stopping occasionally to scrape down the work bowl. Pour into a large bowl. Add the beans, the remaining tomato, celery, avocado, onion, cumin, and coriander. Mix well. Serve over the rice. Season with salt to taste.

Wild Rice and Barley Pilaf

See photo facing page 45.

YIELD: 8 SERVINGS

This dish is nutritious and high in fiber. Make sure to soak the barley and wild rice a full 24 hours.

1 cup barley

1 cup wild rice

3 cups water

4 cups finely chopped fresh spinach

2½ cups thinly sliced portobello mushroom caps

2 yellow bell peppers, diced

1 cup balsamic vinegar

¾ cup tamari

2 avocados, chopped

½ red onion, thinly sliced

Soak the barley and rice in the water in a large glass bowl for 24 hours. Drain and rinse. Transfer to a large bowl with all the remaining ingredients and mix well.

RAW STUFFED PEPPERS: *(See photo facing page 45.)* Slice off the tops of 8 bell peppers and scoop out the seeds. Fill each pepper with the Wild Rice and Barley Pilaf and serve.

Bean Burros

These burros are so delicious and filling that it almost makes you sad that you can only eat one.

¾ cup dried adzuki beans

1 tablespoon ground cumin

½ cup Bragg Liquid Aminos

2½ avocados

½ red onion, sliced

½ cup water

¼ cup tamari

6 red cabbage leaves

3 cups alfalfa sprouts

6 cherry tomatoes, halved

Soak the beans in enough water to cover in a medium bowl for 24 hours. Drain and rinse. Repeat with fresh water for another 24 hours. Drain and rinse. Transfer to a food processor. Process to a paste. Transfer to a medium bowl. Stir in the cumin and Bragg Liquid Aminos. Fold in the avocados. Set aside.

Marinate the onion in the water and tamari for 1 hour. Drain and discard the marinade.

To make the burros, place one-sixth of the bean mixture into each cabbage leaf and spread it with a spoon to cover the entire leaf. Top with ½ cup of the alfalfa sprouts. Add 2 or 3 slices of marinated onion and 2 cherry tomato halves. Roll up burrito-style.

California Roll

See photo facing page 69.

YIELD: 1 SERVING

This recipe is for the sushi lover.

1 sheet nori

½ cup Almond Pâté (page 50; optional)

1 cup alfalfa sprouts

3 thin slices avocado

2 thin slices red bell pepper

½ cup shredded carrots

¼ cup tamari (optional)

Place the nori on the countertop. Spread the optional Almond Pâté on the nori. Place the sprouts on one end of the nori. Top with the avocado, red bell pepper, and carrots.

Roll the nori into a tight roll. If the nori starts to crack, wet your fingers with a little water and tap the crack to seal it. Seal the edge of the nori in the same way so it does not unroll. Slice the roll diagonally into 4 pieces. Serve with the optional tamari for dipping.

Zucchini Pasta with Raw Marinara Sauce

YIELD: 4 TO 6 SERVINGS

With a few zucchini and a little trick up your sleeve, you will always be able to make a quick raw meal using zucchini as pasta.

RAW MARINARA SAUCE

½ cup sun-dried tomatoes (not oil-packed)

1 cup water

1 tablespoon plus 1½ teaspoons honey

2 teaspoons nama shoyu

½ teaspoon garlic powder

½ teaspoon onion powder

4 cups chopped Roma tomatoes

1 cup chopped kalamata olives

1 cup chopped green olives

¼ cup fresh basil leaves, thinly sliced

PASTA

4 large zucchini

½ cup olive oil

Sea salt

To make the Raw Marinara Sauce, soak the sun-dried tomatoes in the water for 2 hours.

Put the soaked tomatoes and the soaking water in a blender with the honey, nama shoyu, garlic powder, and onion powder. Process until smooth, stopping occasionally to scrape down the blender jar. Transfer to a serving bowl. Mix in the Roma tomatoes, olives, and basil.

To make the pasta, peel the zucchini and slice off the ends. Using a vegetable peeler, peel off noodle-shaped slices into a large bowl. Pour in the oil and season with salt to taste. Top with Raw Marinara Sauce.

Falafel in Raw Pita Bread

Falafel is no longer just popular in the Middle East. Everyone loves falafel, so I created this great recipe for the raw world. You can shred some romaine lettuce and serve it on the side with your falafel.

1 cup dried garbanzo beans

1 cup macadamia nuts

1/2 zucchini, chopped

1 tablespoon minced fresh parsley

1 large clove garlic, minced

1/2 teaspoon ground cumin

1/4 teaspoon chili powder

1/4 teaspoon minced fresh oregano leaves

1/4 cup olive oil

1/2 teaspoon sea salt or more to taste

1 teaspoon chopped fresh mint leaves

1/8 teaspoon cayenne

Falafel Bread (recipe follows)

Soak the beans in enough water to cover for 12 hours. Drain and rinse. Put the beans in a blender with the macadamias. Process until the beans are chopped and the mixture is well combined, stopping occasionally to scrape down the blender jar. (The mixture will be dry.)

Add the zucchini. Process again until well mixed. Add the parsley, garlic, cumin, chili powder, and oregano. Process again until well mixed. Add the oil, salt, mint, and cayenne. Process again until well combined.

Form the mixture into 1½-inch balls with your hands. Place them on a dehydrator tray. Dehydrate at 155 degrees F for 12 hours.

Falafel Bread

YIELD: 12 PITAS

½ cup wheat berries, sprouted (see How to Sprout, page 12)

2 cups almond milk

1 cup ground flaxseeds

½ cup macadamia nuts

¼ cup fresh basil leaves

¼ cup sunflower seeds

¼ yellow onion, chopped

1 tablespoon flaxseed oil

1 tablespoon chopped garlic

Put all the ingredients in a food processor. Process until the mixture forms a smooth, creamy dough, stopping occasionally to scrape down the work bowl.

Coat the dehydrator trays with olive oil. Set aside. With a rolling pin, roll out ½ cup of the dough into a 4- to 5-inch circle. Repeat with the remaining dough. Place the rounds on the prepared trays. Dehydrate at 118 degrees F for 12 hours. Refrigerate until serving.

Zucchini Boats

YIELD: 8 SERVINGS

This is another Italian classic that we brought over to the raw world.

CURRY SAUCE

1 cup cashews

2 tomatoes, chopped

1 cup water

1 tablespoon agave nectar

1 tablespoon grated fresh ginger

1 tablespoon lemon juice

1 tablespoon nutritional yeast flakes

2 cloves garlic

1 teaspoon curry powder

1 teaspoon salt (preferably Himalayan)

1 teaspoon ground pepper

FILLING

1 head cauliflower, diced

1 large tomato, diced

1 red bell pepper, diced

¾ cup sliced green onions

½ bunch cilantro leaves, minced

½ cup sunflower sprouts

4 large zucchini

To make the curry sauce, soak the cashews in enough water to cover for 2 hours. Drain. Put them in a blender with all the remaining sauce ingredients. Process until creamy. Set aside.

To make the filling, combine the cauliflower, tomato, bell pepper, green onions, and cilantro in a large bowl. Add the curry sauce and sprouts and toss well.

Slice the zucchini in half lengthwise. With a spoon, remove the seeds to create the boats. To serve, place equal amounts of the filling into each zucchini half.

cheeses

CHAPTER 4

Herb and Seed Cheese

YIELD: 1 CUP

The great thing about seed cheese is that you can take it in many directions. You can use different seeds and various types of nuts and spices to change the flavors. Enjoy taking this seed cheese to an exciting new place.

2 cups sunflower seeds

¾ cup macadamia nuts

½ cup pumpkin seeds

¾ cup lemon juice

¼ cup chopped garlic

¼ cup chopped fresh rosemary

1 tablespoon plus 1½ teaspoons chopped fresh ginger

1 tablespoon sea salt

Soak the sunflower seeds, macadamias, and pumpkin seeds in separate bowls in enough water to cover for 12 hours. Drain and rinse. Put them in a food processor with all the remaining ingredients. Process into a smooth spread, stopping occasionally to scrape down the work bowl. Stored in a covered container in the refrigerator, Herb and Seed Cheese will keep for 2 weeks.

Beet and Seed Cheese

YIELD: 1 CUP

Beets are highly nutritious, but many people just don't know how to prepare them. This "cheese" is a unique but tasty way to put them on your table.

¼ cup pumpkin seeds

¼ cup sunflower seeds

½ cup chopped beets

¼ cup chopped carrots

¼ cup water

2 tablespoons Bragg Liquid Aminos

2 tablespoons chopped garlic

Soak the pumpkin seeds and the sunflower seeds in separate bowls in enough water to cover for 8 to 10 hours or overnight. Drain and rinse. Set aside.

Put the remaining ingredients in a food processor. Process until well mixed, stopping occasionally to scrape down the work bowl. Add the seeds. Process again until smooth, stopping occasionally to scrape down the work bowl. Stored in a covered container in the refrigerator, Beet and Seed Cheese will keep for 2 weeks.

Cashew Cheddar Cheese

YIELD: 2 CUPS

A Cheddar cheese dip is great to serve at any party. This recipe keeps everyone coming back for more so make sure you make plenty of it.

2 cups cashews

1½ cups chopped yellow bell pepper

½ cup chopped red bell pepper

1 large clove garlic

1 tablespoon soy lecithin granules

1 tablespoon ground turmeric

1½ teaspoons sea salt

Soak the cashews in enough water to cover for 1 hour. Drain and rinse. Put them in a food processor. Process for 10 minutes or until smooth and creamy, stopping occasionally to scrape down the work bowl.

Add the remaining ingredients. Process for another 5 minutes, or until smooth and creamy, stopping occasionally to scrape down the work bowl. Stored in a covered container in the refrigerator, Cashew Cheddar Cheese will keep for 2 weeks.

from Karyn's Fresh Corner

Nutty Pimiento Cheese

YIELD: 2 CUPS

Pimiento cheese originated in the South in the early 1900s, and it sure has come a long way. Enjoy this recipe as a spread, in a salad, or as a dip.

2 cups cashews

1½ pimientos, chopped

¼ cup water

2 teaspoons cayenne, plus more to taste

1 tablespoon lime juice

1½ teaspoons sea salt

1 clove garlic

Soak the cashews in enough water to cover for 1 hour. Drain and rinse. Transfer them to a blender. Process for 8 to 10 minutes, or until smooth and creamy, stopping occasionally to scrape down the blender jar.

Add all the remaining ingredients. Process again until smooth and creamy, stopping occasionally to scrape down the blender jar. Stored in a covered container in the refrigerator, Nutty Pimiento Cheese will keep for 2 weeks.

snacks

CHAPTER 5

Sesame-Lime Hummus

YIELD: 2 CUPS

There are so many different kinds of hummus on the market, it's hard to pick a favorite. But I can tell you one thing: Mine is the best.

1 cup water

¾ cup sesame seeds

¼ cup lime juice

¼ cup olive oil

¼ cup sunflower seeds

1½ teaspoons chopped fresh ginger

1½ teaspoons sea salt

½ teaspoon cayenne

1 teaspoon olive oil (optional)

Paprika, for garnish

Put the water, sesame seeds, lime juice, ¼ cup of the oil, sunflower seeds, ginger, salt, and cayenne in a blender. Process on high speed for 1 to 2 minutes, or until smooth and creamy, stopping occasionally to scrape down the blender jar. Transfer to a serving bowl. Top with the optional oil and paprika if desired.

Bruschetta

YIELD: ABOUT 3 CUPS

This ubiquitous appetizer is always served raw, but the raw White Bread makes a delightful difference.

- 2½ cups minced Roma tomatoes
- ¼ cup chopped fresh basil leaves
- 2 tablespoons minced garlic
- 2 tablespoons olive oil
- ¾ teaspoon sea salt
- **White Bread** (page 70)

Combine all of the ingredients in a large bowl and mix well. Let marinate for 2 hours before serving. Or spread the mixture on dehydrator trays and dehydrate at 118 degrees F for 2 hours. Serve on White Bread.

Nacho Chips

YIELD: 5 TO 6 SERVINGS

Keeping these chips around will always ensure that you have a quick, healthy snack. You can use these with any of the cheeses in this book or with your favorite dip.

- 3½ cups flaxseeds
- 4 cups chopped yellow bell peppers
- 4 cups fresh or frozen corn kernels, thawed, if frozen
- 2 cups sunflower seeds
- 1 cup chopped yellow onion
- ¼ cup garlic cloves
- 2 tablespoons paprika
- 2 tablespoons chili powder
- 2 tablespoons ground turmeric
- Sea salt

Put the flaxseeds in a blender or food processor. Process into a powder. Transfer to a bowl and set aside.

Put the peppers, corn, sunflower seeds, onion, cloves, paprika, and chili powder in the blender. Process until smooth and creamy, stopping occasionally to scrape down the blender jar. Transfer to a large bowl and fold in the ground flaxseeds. Season with salt to taste.

Line the dehydrator trays with nonstick dehydrator sheets. Spread the mixture onto the sheets and mark triangle shapes with a knife. Dehydrate at 118 degrees F for 4 hours. Flip onto the trays and dehydrate for another 12 hours. Break up into chips.

Onion Crisps

YIELD: 4 CUPS

Onions have a very strong smell that lingers on the skin. After slicing or chopping onions, wash your hands in cold water, and then rub them with salt or vinegar to remove the smell from your hands.

½ cup cashews

½ cup walnuts

3½ pounds yellow onions, thinly sliced

¾ cup nutritional yeast flakes

1 tablespoon plus 1½ teaspoons sea salt

Put the cashews and walnuts in a food processor. Pulse 2 or 3 times, or just until the nuts are broken into small chunks. Transfer them to a large bowl and add all the remaining ingredients. Mix until the onions are coated with the nut mixture.

Spread the mixture in a thin layer on dehydrator trays. Dehydrate at 110 degrees F for 24 hours. For a crunchier texture, dehydrate for another 12 hours. Stored in a covered container in a cool, dry place, Onion Crisps will keep indefinitely.

Almond-Berry Muffins *(top)* **and Almond-Carrot Muffins** *(bottom), page 16*

California Roll, *page 54*

Wheat Berry Crackers

YIELD: 20 CRACKERS

This recipe was originally created from leftover wheat berries from Rejuvelac (page 13). Nothing is ever wasted in a raw food kitchen. If you are using Rejuvelac leftovers, you will need almost no additional water in this recipe.

2¼ cup wheat berries

¼ cup Bragg Liquid Aminos

¼ cup water

1 tablespoon garlic powder

Soak the wheat berries in enough water to cover for 24 hours. Drain and rinse. Transfer them to a blender with the remaining ingredients. Process until the mixture is the consistency of thick pancake batter, stopping occasionally to scrape down the blender jar.

Spread the batter evenly on the dehydrator trays. With a butter knife, mark the batter into the desired cracker sizes and shapes so it will be easier to break apart after it's dehydrated. Dehydrate at 110 degrees F for 8 to 12 hours, or until crispy. Stored in a covered container in a cool, dry place, Wheat Berry Crackers will keep indefinitely.

White Bread

The name is only a reflection of the color. Don't confuse this nutrient-packed raw bread with the nutritionally void white variety in supermarkets. If your dehydrator is small and you have leftover dough, refrigerate it, and dehydrate another time.

3 cups pearl barley

1¾ cups almonds

½ cup agave nectar

½ cup flaxseeds

¼ cup garlic

¼ cup olive oil

2 tablespoons chopped fresh dill

1 tablespoon sea salt

Soak the barley and almonds in separate bowls in enough water to cover for 12 hours. Drain and rinse. Transfer to a food processor with all the remaining ingredients. Process until the mixture forms a dough, stopping occasionally to scrape down the work bowl.

Spread the dough evenly on the dehydrator trays with your hands to ¼-inch thickness. With a butter knife, mark the dough into bread-slice shapes so it will be easier to break apart after it's dehydrated. Dehydrate at 120 degrees F for 18 hours, or until desired crispness.

Wrapped in plastic wrap and refrigerated, the dough will keep for 1 month. Stored in a covered container in a cool, dry place, White Bread will keep indefinitely.

Honey-Kale Chips

YIELD: 3 TO 4 SERVINGS

Not many people know how delicious kale can be until they try these kale chips. This is a great alternative to potato chips.

1 cup honey

1 cup lemon juice

1 cup extra-virgin olive oil

1 pound kale, stems removed

Wrap the dehydrator trays in plastic wrap.

Whisk the honey, lemon juice, and oil in a large bowl.

Make sure the kale is dry. Dip the kale leaves in the honey mixture, shake off any excess, and place them on the prepared dehydrator trays. Dehydrate at 118 degrees F for 8 hours, checking occasionally for the desired crispness.

Granola Bars

YIELD: 10 BARS

With most dehydrated snacks, you have some flexibility in how long you dehydrate them. The longer these Granola Bars are dehydrated, the crispier they will be.

2 cups buckwheat

1 cup cold water

6 cups rolled oats

2½ cups honey

2 cups sliced almonds

2 cups raisins

1½ cups almond butter

Soak the buckwheat in the water in a large bowl for about 2 hours, or until all the water is absorbed. Add all the remaining ingredients and mix well.

Line the dehydrator trays with nonstick dehydrator sheets. Spread the mixture evenly on the sheets to ½-inch thickness. With a knife, slice the dough to form 10 equal-sized granola bars. Dehydrate at 115 degrees F for 4 hours. Flip the bars over onto the trays and remove the nonstick dehydrator sheets. Dehydrate for another 6 hours, occasionally checking for desired crispness. Stored in a covered container in the refrigerator or other cool, dry place, Granola Bars will keep indefinitely.

CHAPTER 6

desserts

Coconut Pudding

YIELD: 4 SERVINGS

When you have a taste for something sweet, this is a quick and simple way to satisfy that craving.

3 cups coconut meat

1¾ cups coconut water

¼ cup agave nectar

Put the coconut, coconut water, and agave nectar in a blender. Process for 5 minutes, or until smooth and creamy, stopping occasionally to scrape down the blender jar. Stored in a covered container in the refrigerator, Coconut Pudding will keep for 10 days.

Oaty Carob Cake

YIELD: 12 SERVINGS

This is a very rich and filling dessert. Be sure to keep it refrigerated.

6¾ cups rolled oats

2 cups carob powder

1½ cups agave nectar

1¼ cups coconut water

1 cup almond butter

¼ cup plus 1 tablespoon ground cinnamon

½ cup water

Combine the oats, 1 cup of the carob powder, 1 cup of the agave nectar, coconut water, almond butter, and cinnamon in a large bowl with your hands until the mixture becomes thick and claylike. Pack it into a 9 x 9-inch baking pan.

To make the frosting, put the remaining 1 cup of the carob powder, the remaining ½ cup of agave nectar, and the water in a blender. Process until smooth and creamy, stopping occasionally to scrape down the blender jar. Frost the cake. Refrigerate until serving.

Apple Ambrosia

YIELD: 4 SERVINGS

This recipe will really satisfy your palate with the classic combination of sweet and sour.

¼ cup honey

¼ cup molasses

¼ cup tahini

¼ cup chopped walnuts

2 tablespoons almond butter

2 tablespoons raw cashew butter

2 Granny Smith apples, peeled, cored, and cut into wedges

Combine the honey, molasses, tahini, walnuts, almond butter, and cashew butter in a large bowl. Place the apple wedges on a dessert plate. Pour the walnut mixture over the apple wedges.

Berry Delight Parfaits

Making this in advance ensures you'll always have a healthful breakfast or snack on hand.

2 cups cashews

3 cups pitted dates

¼ cup raw honey, maple syrup, agave nectar, or other sweetener of your choice

½ teaspoon vanilla extract

1½ cups pecans, plus more for garnish

1 pound strawberries or blueberries or a mixture

Karyn's Granola (page 15) **or flaxseeds, for garnish**

Soak the cashews in enough water to cover for 5 hours. Soak the dates in enough water to cover in a separate bowl for 2 hours.

Drain and rinse the cashews and transfer them to a blender with the honey and vanilla extract. Process until smooth, stopping occasionally to scrape down the blender jar. If mixture seems too thick, add water 1 tablespoon at a time and process again. Transfer the cashew cream to a medium bowl. Wash and dry the blender jar.

Drain and rinse the dates and transfer them to the blender with 1½ cups of the pecans and ½ cup of water. Process until the pecans are completely broken up, stopping occasionally to scrape down the blender jar. Transfer to a medium bowl. Wash and dry the blender jar.

Put the berries in the blender. Process until they are chopped and mixed well. Do not process into a liquid.

Layer the date mixture, berries, and the cashew cream equally among six parfait glasses. Chill for 3 to 5 hours. Garnish with chopped pecans, Karyn's Granola, or flaxseeds.

Tirawmisu

YIELD: 15 SERVINGS

Tiramisu is an Italian dessert, and it is the perfect ending to any meal. This version freezes well, so you can make it in advance and thaw when needed.

COOKIES

1¼ cups pitted dates

3 cups walnuts

FILLING

2 cups cashews, soaked for 1 hour (see Soak Your Nuts, page 11)

1 cup coconut water

½ cup agave nectar

2 tablespoons maca root powder

WHITE SAUCE

2 cups cashews, soaked for 1 hour (see Soak Your Nuts, page 11)

½ cup agave nectar

½ cup coconut water

½ teaspoon vanilla extract

CHOCOLATE CREAM

2 cups coconut meat

1 cup raw cacao powder

½ cup plus 2 tablespoons agave nectar

½ cup coconut water

1½ teaspoons coconut oil

Raw cacao powder for garnish

To make the cookies, soak the dates in enough water to cover for 24 hours. Drain. Put them in a blender. Process until smooth, stopping occasionally to scrape down the blender jar. Transfer to a large bowl.

Wash and dry the blender jar. Add the walnuts. Process until the walnuts are chopped and they release some of their oil and the consistency is thick and slightly moist. Add them to the dates and mix well to form a dough. Divide the dough into 5 equal parts. Roll each part into a 7-inch-long roll with your hands. Dehydrate at 118 degrees F for 12 hours. Place the cookie rolls in a 15 x 11-inch baking pan.

To make the filling, drain and rinse the cashews. Put them in a blender with the coconut water, agave nectar, and maca root powder. Process until the consistency resembles mashed potatoes, stopping occasionally to scrape down the blender jar. Pour the filling over the cookie layer in the baking pan. Wash and dry the blender jar.

To make the white sauce, drain and rinse the cashews. Put them in the blender with the agave nectar, coconut water, and vanilla extract. Process until smooth, stopping occasionally to scrape down the blender jar. Pour the white sauce over the filling.

To make the chocolate cream, wash and dry the blender jar. Put the coconut meat, cacao powder, agave nectar, coconut water, and coconut oil in the blender. Process until thoroughly blended. Pour over the white sauce.

Sprinkle with cacao powder. Freeze for 2 hours before serving. Cover and store leftovers in the freezer.

VARIATION: Double the cookie recipe and use the extra cookies for garnish or to serve on the side.

Banana Pudding

YIELD: 4 SERVINGS

This is a raw twist to a Southern classic.

- 1¼ cups cashews
- ¾ cup water
- ¼ cup honey
- 1½ teaspoons vanilla extract
- 1 tablespoon flaxseed oil
- 3 tablespoons flaxseeds
- 2 bananas, sliced

Put the cashews, water, honey, vanilla extract, and oil in a blender. Process for 5 minutes, or until smooth and creamy, stopping occasionally to scrape down the blender jar.

Sprinkle 1 teaspoon of the flaxseeds in a serving dish or cup. Add a few banana slices, about ½ cup of the cashew mixture, another layer of banana slices, and another teaspoon of flaxseeds. Repeat with the remaining ingredients.

Nutty Flax Cupcakes

YIELD: 12 CUPCAKES

No matter what the age of the recipient, cupcakes are always a hit.

- **2½ cups pecans**
- **2½ cups walnuts**
- **2½ cups rolled oats**
- **1¼ cups flaxseeds**
- **1 cup agave nectar**
- **¼ cup plus 2 tablespoons coconut butter**
- **1 tablespoon vanilla extract**

In a large blender, process the pecans and walnuts into a fine powder. Transfer the nut mixture to a large bowl.

Put the oats and flaxseeds in the blender. Process to a powder. Transfer to the bowl with the pecans and walnuts. Add the agave nectar, coconut butter, and vanilla extract. Mix with your hands until a dough forms. Form ½ cup of the dough into a ball and place it in on a dehydrator tray. Repeat with the remaining dough. Dehydrate at 115 degrees F for 24 hours. Stored in a covered container in the refrigerator, Nutty Flax Cupcakes will keep for 3 weeks.

Cranberry Cookies

YIELD: 12 SERVINGS

If there's such a thing as beautiful cookies, these certainly qualify, thanks to the dried cranberries.

10 cups cashews

2 cups sweetened dried cranberries

1½ cups honey

¼ cup plus 2 tablespoons almond butter

Put the cashews in a blender. Process into a fine powder. Transfer the cashews to a large bowl.

Add all the remaining ingredients and mix well. Spread the mixture 1½ inches thick on dehydrator trays. Dehydrate at 118 degrees F for 48 hours. Cut into the desired sizes and shapes.

Carob-Pecan Cake

This is one of the first recipes I ever developed. The cake is sweet and will satisfy every chocolate lover's craving.

6 cups chopped pecans

1½ cups carob powder

1 cup almond butter

1 cup honey

2 tablespoons ground cinnamon

2 tablespoons vanilla extract

Combine all the ingredients in a large bowl. Mix well. Press into a 13 x 9-inch glass baking dish. Refrigerate until chilled before serving.

Apple Pie

You can serve this pie with a scoop of hempseed ice cream and have yourself an American classic with a raw twist.

CRUST

1 cup pitted dates

1 cup almonds

1 cup pecans

1 cup shredded dried coconut

FILLING

4 cups raisins

3 Granny Smith apples, peeled and diced

3 red apples, peeled and diced

2 tablespoons lime juice

1 teaspoon ground cinnamon

FROSTING

2 cups cashews, soaked for 30 minutes
   (see Soak Your Nuts, page 11)

$\frac{1}{2}$ cup water

$\frac{1}{4}$ cup honey

To make the crust, soak the dates in enough water to cover for 1 hour.

Meanwhile, put the almonds and pecans in a food processor. Process into a fine powder. Transfer to a large bowl.

Drain the dates. Put them in the blender. Process until well chopped. Add them to the nut mixture with the coconut. Mix well with your hands and transfer to a 10-inch pie pan. Press the mixture into the bottom and up the sides of the pan. Dehydrate at 115 degrees for 2 hours.

To make the filling, put 3 cups of the raisins in a blender. Process to a paste, stopping occasionally to scrape down the blender jar. Transfer to a large bowl with the apples. Stir in the remaining 1 cup of the raisins, lime juice, and cinnamon. Pour the filling into the pie crust and smooth the top with the back of a spoon. Wash and dry the blender jar.

To make the frosting, drain and rinse the cashews. Put them in the blender with the water and honey. Process until smooth and creamy, stopping occasionally to scrape down the blender jar. Spread the frosting evenly over the top of the pie. Refrigerate for 4 hours before serving.

German "Chocolate" Cake

This is a wonderful cake for birthday parties or bake sales.

8 cups pitted dates

5 cups macadamia nuts, finely chopped

5 cups walnuts, finely chopped

3½ cups shredded dried coconut

2 cups carob powder

½ cup tahini

3 tablespoons vanilla extract

2 cups pecans

1½ cups water

Soak the dates in enough water to cover for 1 hour. Drain. Transfer them to a blender. Process to a paste, stopping occasionally to scrape down the blender jar. Put 2 cups of the date paste in a large bowl. Add the macadamias, walnuts, 3 cups of the coconut, 1 cup of the carob powder, tahini, and vanilla extract. Mix well. Spread into a 10-inch cake pan and smooth the top with the back of a spoon. Remove the cake from the pan and place on a serving plate.

To make the frosting, add the pecans, water, and the remaining 1 cup of carob powder to the remaining dates in the blender. Process until smooth and creamy, stopping occasionally to scrape down the blender jar. Spread the frosting over the top and sides of the cake. Sprinkle the remaining ½ cup of coconut on top. Keep refrigerated.

Yin-Yang Cheesecake

YIELD: 12 SERVINGS

This cake is a favorite at my store.

CRUST

2 cups pecans

½ cup honey

¼ cup raw cacao powder

CHOCOLATE FILLING

4 cups cashews, soaked for 2 hours (see Soak Your Nuts, page 11)

2 cups cacao butter

¾ cup honey

¼ cup raw cacao powder

VANILLA FILLING

4 cups cashews, soaked for 2 hours (see Soak Your Nuts, page 11)

2 cups cacao butter

¾ cup honey

2 tablespoons vanilla extract

TOPPING

3 cups pecans

½ cup cacao nibs

To make the crust, put the pecans in a blender. Process into small chunks. Transfer to a medium bowl. Add the cacao powder and honey. Mix well. Press the mixture into the bottom and up the sides of a 10-inch springform pan. Set aside. Wash and dry the blender jar.

To make the chocolate filling, drain and rinse the cashews. Transfer them to the blender. Break up the cacao butter into small chunks with a knife and add them to the blender with the honey and cacao powder. Process on high speed until smooth and creamy and the consistency of thick pudding, stopping occasionally to scrape down the blender jar. Pour the mixture evenly into the crust. Smooth the top with a spatula. Set aside. Wash and dry the blender jar.

To make the vanilla filling, drain and rinse the cashews. Transfer them to the blender. Break up the cacao butter into small chunks with a knife and add them to the blender with the honey and vanilla extract. Process on high speed until smooth and creamy and the consistency of thick pudding, stopping occasionally to scrape down the blender jar. Pour the mixture evenly over the chocolate filling. Smooth the top with a spatula. Freeze for 10 minutes.

Meanwhile, wash and dry the blender jar and make the topping. Put the pecans in the blender. Process until the pecans are broken up and still chunky. Transfer the pecans to a medium bowl. Stir in the cacao nibs. Remove the cake from the freezer. Remove the side of the springform pan. Cover the top and sides of the cake with the pecan mixture. Freeze for another 2 hours before serving or store the cake in the refrigerator.

Spaceballs

The great thing about this recipe is that you don't have to dehydrate it unless you want a chewier texture. If you do, dehydrate it at 118 degrees F for 2 hours.

2 cups pitted dates

12 figs, stems removed

2 cups hempseed butter

1 cup pecans

1 cup raisins

1 cup walnuts

⅓ cup carob powder

1 tablespoon spirulina

2 cups shredded dried coconut

Soak the dates in enough water to cover for 4 hours. Soak the figs in enough water to cover in a separate bowl for 2 hours.

Drain the dates. Transfer them to a blender. Process to a paste, stopping occasionally to scrape down the blender jar. Drain the figs. Add them to the blender with the dates, along with the hempseed butter, pecans, raisins, walnuts, carob powder, and spirulina. Process until the mixture reaches the consistency of cookie dough, stopping occasionally to scrape down the blender jar. If the mixture seems too thick, add water 1 tablespoon at a time and process again.

Form the mixture into 1-inch balls with your hands. Roll them in the coconut until well coated. Stored in a covered container in the refrigerator, Spaceballs will keep for 3 weeks.

Zesty Lemon Cheesecake

YIELD: 8 SERVINGS

This cheesecake is so creamy it will melt in your mouth; no one will believe you when you say this is raw.

CRUST

2 cups walnuts

1 cup pitted dates, soaked for 1 hour

FILLING

3 cups cashews, soaked for 1 hour (see Soak Your Nuts, page 11)

1¾ cups agave nectar

1½ cups lemon zest (from 12 lemons)

1¼ cups coconut oil

1 cup lemon juice

To make the crust, put the walnuts in a food processor. Process into a fine powder. Transfer to a medium bowl.

Drain the dates. Transfer them to a blender. Process to a paste, stopping occasionally to scrape down the blender jar. Add to the walnuts. Mix well. Transfer the mixture to a 10-inch pie pan. Press it evenly into the bottom of the pan. Do not spread it up the sides of the pan. Dehydrate at 110 degrees F for 3 hours. Wash and dry the blender jar.

To make the filling, drain and rinse the cashews. Transfer them to the blender with the agave nectar, 1 cup of the lemon zest, oil, and lemon juice. Process until smooth and creamy. Pour into the pie crust. Spread it evenly, smoothing the top with the back of a spoon. Sprinkle the remaining ½ cup of the lemon zest on top. Freeze for 12 hours.

Take the cheesecake out of the freezer 1 hour before serving.

Lemon Drop Cookies

YIELD: 2 DOZEN COOKIES

These lemony cookies will satisfy everybody's sweet tooth—without being too sweet.

3 cups cashews

2 cups macadamia nuts

2 cups water

1 cup honey

1 cup maple syrup

1 cup pine nuts

1 tablespoon vanilla extract

1 teaspoon flaxseed oil

3 cups lemon juice

Put the cashews, macadamias, water, honey, maple syrup, pine nuts, vanilla extract, and oil in a blender. Process until well combined, stopping occasionally to scrape down the blender jar. Add the lemon juice. Process until well combined and smooth.

Form 1 tablespoon of the dough into the shape of a chocolate candy kiss. Place on a nonstick dehydrator sheet. Repeat with the remaining dough. Dehydrate at 110 degrees F for 24 hours. Remove the cookies from the nonstick dehydrator sheets and transfer them to the dehydrator tray. Dehydrate for another 24 hours.

Vanilla Ice Cream

YIELD: 1 QUART

Vanilla ice cream is a must in every household in the summertime.

2½ cups Nut Milk (page 10) **or prepared nut milk**

1 cup coconut meat

¾ cup honey

½ cup coconut water

¼ cup vanilla extract

Put all the ingredients in a blender. Process on high speed until smooth and creamy, stopping occasionally to scrape down the blender jar. Pour into an ice-cream maker and follow the manufacturer's instructions.

We All Scream

You don't have to have an ice-cream maker to make ice cream. Instead, freeze your ice-cream mixture in ice cube trays. When it's time to serve, put the frozen ice cream cubes in a blender or a food processor, and process until creamy.

Hempseed Ice Cream

YIELD: 1 QUART

This ice cream is so rich and creamy. Even when frozen for more than a couple days, it still scoops easily because of the high fat content—all of it good fats— from the hempseeds.

- **2 cups hempseeds**
- **1¾ cups maple syrup**
- **1 cup water**
- **½ cup coconut meat**
- **¼ cup coconut oil**

Put all the ingredients in a blender. Process on high speed until smooth and creamy, stopping occasionally to scrape down the blender jar. Pour into an ice-cream maker and follow the manufacturer's instructions.

Mango Ice Cream

YIELD: 1 QUART

You can use fresh or frozen mangoes for this recipe. (Whenever you have mango that is starting to become overripe, peel the mango, slice it, and freeze it so you'll be prepared.)

5 cups chopped fresh or frozen mangoes (5 to 6 mangoes)

1 cup almond milk

¾ cup honey or agave nectar

½ cup coconut butter

¼ cup vanilla extract

Put all the ingredients in a blender. Process on high speed until smooth and creamy, stopping occasionally to scrape down the blender jar. Pour into an ice-cream maker and follow the manufacturer's instructions.

Curry Ice Cream

YIELD: 1 QUART

Curry is admittedly an intriguing flavor for ice cream. It is also delicious.

2 pitted dates, soaked for 2 hours

½ cup coconut meat

½ cup raisins

1 tablespoon agave nectar

1½ teaspoons curry powder

Drain the dates, reserving about 3 tablespoons of the soak water. Transfer the dates and the reserved soak water to a blender with all the remaining ingredients. Process on high speed until smooth and creamy, stopping occasionally to scrape down the blender jar. Pour into an ice-cream maker and follow the manufacturer's instructions.

Strawberry Ice Cream

YIELD: 2½ QUARTS

This recipe is a very popular treat for children and grownups.

- **8 cups frozen strawberries**
- **2 cups almonds**
- **2 cups honey**
- **1½ cups coconut butter or coconut meat**
- **½ cup vanilla extract**

Put all the ingredients in a blender. Process on high speed until smooth and creamy, stopping occasionally to scrape down the blender jar. Pour into an ice-cream maker and follow the manufacturer's instructions.

index